W9-AYZ-256

Smoke of My Own Breath

For Marry & Ray —
Treasured friends —
Love,
[signature] 4-27-02

SMOKE OF
MY OWN BREATH

David Hilton

 Garlic Press

St. Louis, Missouri

ACKNOWLEDGMENTS

Some of these poems appeared previously in the following journals:

ABRAXAS: "The Clothes Pile"
EXQUISITE CORPSE: "Cherry"; "Dave's Circus"; "First High"; "Through the Wall"
FLOATING ISLAND: "'Honey Hush'"
5 AM: "The Bait" (titled "The Plan")
LONG SHOT: "Marge Barnes"
MINNESOTA REVIEW: "Big C Suite"
POET LORE: "Love Life"; "The Melmac Year"; "The Old Hog Farm"
POETRY MOTEL: "Tijuana"
POETRY NORTHWEST: "Dollar Bill"; "17020 Via Pasatiempo"; "Warmth"
THE REAPER: "'Pachuco Hop'"
THE TALKING RIVER REVIEW: "The Thing"

The following poems also appeared in the chapbook *No Relation to the Hotel* (Coffee House Press, 1990): "Big C Suite," Dollar Bill," "The Melmac Year," "'Pachuco Hop,'" "The Piano."

"The Melmac Year" was included in *Up Late: American Poetry Since 1970* (Four Walls Eight Windows Press, 1987).

Thanks to Al Young for his *Kinds of Blue*, the book that helped me tune in the far-distant station for "'Honey Hush'" and "'Pachuco Hop.'"

Special thanks to David Clewell, foreman on this job.

ISBN: 0-964-3009-4-X

For my brothers John (1944–2000) and Paul, fellow foot soldiers throughout the long Battle of San Lorenzo,

and for Joanne, who tended the wounds

TABLE OF CONTENTS

The smoke of my own breath,
echoes, ripples, buzz'd whispers, love-root, silk-thread,
crotch and vine . . .

—Walt Whitman, "Song of Myself"

WARMTH

The liquid glowed thick
in the cold morning
in the glasses purple-frosted
with pinup girls and storks.

Lipstick kissing the rims,
cigarette butts leaching amber
in the sweet oily bottom
sips of the highballs,

manhattans, collins, sours—
and the crusty-eyed boy
in pajamas that mittened his feet
drank them all down in turn.

Thus he warmed himself
before reaching the long wire rod
with the match-flame at its tip
down through the heat grate

to try to light the pilot.
And this way, too, he helped
straighten up the house
before they moaned and awoke.

DOLLAR BILL

Grandma knew the meaning of the dollar's
Mystic Eye. Like her own, it pulled
toward the moon, toward the evil red canals
of Mars, her tidal all-blinding sclera.

Mystic Eye impaled on the pyramid meant
Zoltar, ace Venusian saucer pilot, watched
over us, poor Earth fallen, blackened,
sunk to the bottom of the Galaxy. Zoltar

gave her the Rings of Saturn to sign over
her old-age checks to Daddy Ballard,
founder of the MIGHTY I AM, who climbed
Mount Shasta in a flowing golden robe

and disappeared. The MIGHTY I AM in Oakland
sold Grandma every shape of the color purple
and each week's fifty-cent message from
the Ascended Masters, Saint Germain and

George Washington her favorites. She bought
the huge album of chants, purple cover
embossed with the All-Seeing Eye,
the same one staring out the dollar bill—

and she'd unfold a dollar bill
like a rose out of her change purse
to show me this proof that our Earth
was plunging entirely out of the Universe.

Only Zoltar could save us! She'd say, "Please
chant with me," so I'd put a stack of chant records
on her little plastic Victrola. She lifted
her great weight, stretched her arms north

toward Shasta, gasped, collapsed—that
was how far we'd fallen. Then the first
chant record dropped: *harmonize this house,*
harmonize this house, harmonize this house,

harmonize . . . she and I in unison
until the last record scraped to silence
and we sat in the dark in her purple room
listening for the roar of star-burning engines.

GREAT-AUNT GERTRUDE

1.

Old Great-Aunt Gertrude was always rumored
to be . . . but then their faces turned away,
heads lowered, mouths moved closer
as if to kiss, and their talk became
the brushing of slippers on linoleum,
combs sliding through heavy hair,
dresses smoothed over silk underwear.

Aunt Gertrude, the old maid,
so homely; and poor, dried up, sad,
having to feed and keep clean
a slowly dying crazy rich man
for room and board, and herself
not always . . . not really quite . . . *hush* . . .
and their whispering began.

2.

So the boy had to worry why he
was her favorite. Every Christmas Eve,
the only day she was seen,
at the other sister's (the banker's wife),
she had made for him the strangest book—
heavy pages stitched together
with all colors of the toughest yarn;
and cuttings of brightest rags,
of tinfoil and seed labels and magazines,
catalogs and greeting cards and maps,
bits of string and ribbons,
even some pennies and buttons

and ringlets of gray hair
and whole candy wrappers
all glued to the pages, *were* the pages,
without an open or rough seam or edge or overlap
or, it seemed to him, the least confusion.

3.

Weighted with beautiful faces—Santa, Indians,
cherubs, movie stars, cover girls, Jesus—
the book lay on the rich aunt's Persian rug.
The boy curled around it, over it,
nearly embracing it, lost to the other presents.
He lifted its thick, stiff pages,
tracing the textures as if blind,
inhaling a musty glue-smell mixed
with sachet of spice-dust, petals, mothwings.

Before they left he usually got up
the courage to look in her eyes
and murmur "Thank you."

It was Aunt Gertrude's only gift
to *anybody*—poor Aunt Gertrude, never,
even as a girl, quite . . . well . . . all there,
who worked the whole year every year
creating that crazy book
for the silent, peculiar boy.

THE PIANO

No one played it but me, alone
in the fringed, brocaded living room,
pounding out the distances between
the black bones and the white,
between Grandpa's moans that shook
and shuddered down the stairs
and his trapped cries that broke
and fell like that small bird, the mud-
molded, shadow-stunned thing that had seen
in the half-open attic window
an endless gray sky.

All morning I had helped Grandma chase it.
Her windmilling broom
knocked it from walls to rafters.
I thought it was trying to find
a way into my upreaching hands,
but the birdscreams stopped and I heard
Grandma wailing how death
had entered the house.
I ran to pick it up. Feathers stuck out
blood-slick, thistly, cold—
they would not smooth. Then asthma
clenched my chest. I knelt,
head racked back, wheezing within
a generation's dust flying free.

That was when Grandpa went upstairs
to stay in bed. The women turned him
into whispers, into a word
they could not ever say.
And I never saw him again.

The piano was all mine
in the deserted living room,
and mine the huge warm cave
under the piano where Grandpa
had always read the Sunday funnies to me,
where he changed me into Popeye and

Buck Rogers and Mandrake the Magician.
Under the piano I was invisible.
Grandpa grabbed for me and missed—
"Where's David? I know he's under here
but I can't see him," hands reaching,
clutching an inch in front of my nose.
"Where is that little devil?" Finally,
led by my laughing, he'd have me and
hug me up and out into the air—
"Ah, now I've got you. Did you think I couldn't find you?"

After Grandpa went away, I'd still
smash on the piano until
they made me stop. Catch me banging
that piano anymore, they said,
and they'd slam the lid shut
and chop my fingers off.
                         So I climbed
down off the stool, as far
down as I could get, and pulled
all the soft blue hammers, the slow-
quieting strings and
quivering heartwood close down
around me, trembling inside them
like the shortest, thinnest wire,
and waited for the women's weeping
to put me, unseen, to sleep.

GLUTEN STEAKS

His grandmother had flown with wise
and harmonious Venusians and returned
from her saucer journeys Vegetarian,
though she and the boy loved meat.

Dinner for the two of them
in her widow's-mite trailer
was invariably gluten steaks.
She couldn't say what these were,

and he didn't care. They were good—
each one a quivery, pearly gray
circular slab of mealy meatlike matter
with sugary brown gravy for sopping.

And if he wanted more, she'd say,
"You know how to open up another can,"
since the steaks came tightly stacked,
gelled in that gravy, in a tin

he could open with a key on which
she'd taught him to wind a perfect spool
of razory steel ribbon. Then the meat
sucked free and slid onto his plate.

And whatever he liked for dessert—
jelly doughnuts and brown-sugar sandwiches the best—
she'd say, "Go on, finish them all—
that's how they eat on Venus."

BIG C SUITE

for "Tommy" Hilton

Mother's last letter said rain—spring
still cold, wind off the bay like ice—
and asked again if I meant to stay
in Maryland, the whole country away,
forever. Then said you finally found out
it's terminal after the surgeon hung up the films
and explained that it's not an infection
you just can't shake, but cancer
spread in the lungs, inoperable
because nothing would be left
except emphysema. "It's the Big C,"
you actually say. "The fucking Big C.
When he snipped it open I could feel
the air rush in, but they give you only
one biopsy, and that was my second."
—Her first letter: "David,
hope and pray
it's not cancer."

• • •

I was nine and we were driving back Sunday from Russian
River, you said "whore" as part of a joke, and I laughed so
hard you said, "I just keep him around to laugh at my jokes,"
and tickled me until I got a bad asthma attack and Mother
said, "Tommy, look what you did to him." That's about all I
remember about that sort of thing.

• • •

Tommy, you stole a wife and me
from a nineteen-year-old Irish tenor called
"my real father," all abstract rumor
like Catholic Beater-Up of Cops, more unknown
than the Devil but for the one secret
sensing I'm sure I had of him:
a fine, pure howl, a keening that rose
from the dark Outside, sleep-music
to the infant whom it roused
and shook without waking. I was twenty
when Grandma showed me the antique
news-photo she'd saved from the *Chronicle*:
beautiful, slouched, sullen, shock-haired
1939 motorcycle punk in Superior Court—
"Thug sentenced for assault," the cut-line said—
my mother seated small next to him,
holding up the child as if even then
it was my job to save her.

• • •

You tore down engines since you were fourteen.
And for a few years after the war,
whenever customers fell for your phantom
valve-jobs, you'd come home and hurl great fistfuls
of dollars to the kitchen floor and shout
"I don't want ALL the money in the world,
just MOST OF IT!"—
and very rich and very drunk,
you'd dance and curse upon your money.

• • •

For a while cobalt burns fresh
air passages, stuns the tumors.
After chemotherapy you're feeling OK,

want to get back to work, but solvent
eating itself in your hot-dip tank
blows up the last TOMMY HILTON'S AUTO AND
　　MACHINE SHOP,
just a rented backyard shed in East Oakland.
"Middle of niggertown," you said, "but the niggers
are better than most white men I can name."
Even in that shed you were *Tommy*
and displayed in its dimestore frame
the DOCTOR OF MOTORS diploma awarded
by Perfect Circle Piston Rings, 1947, when
you bought your first boring bar
and drank cheap Scotch with rich small-timers
and dropped hundred-dollar bills at Golden Gate Fields
and got beaten steadily in the card rooms of Emeryville
and drove home in customers' cars because you didn't have
　　gas money.
Toward the end, you'd lose
at shuffleboard, electric bowling, liars' dice.

　　　　　　　　　　　　• • •

Your mother, Olga,
savage alcoholic, died alone
in the Napa madhouse—
this you wait
all your life to tell me,
how her kisses
were cheap sweet wine
and puke. Olga Brodenheim—
you spell it for me
and swear
she wasn't Jewish.

　　　　　　　　　　　　• • •

Last year before
you died, you asked me
about the name,
has it ever "opened
any doors?" You
told me then
how *Hilton*
got you a prime
weekend table at Tahoe
for Sinatra once
and Wayne Newton,
George Gobel, many others.
I always say, "No,
no relation
to the hotel."

• • •

I'll not be there when you die.
Who will stand at the grave beside your brother,
smart enough to stick with Chevy,
now Parts Manager, and my mother
and her crazy sister and
my two baby brothers, who never got out
("half-brothers, technically," I always explain)?
Will anyone come to see you in the funeral home
except Pete Ostrowky, Oakland's almost-millionaire
auto-upholsterer with the 210 average at
Broadway Bowl in 1953, your pal? No,
Pete won't come, he's a real millionaire now.
Only the woman, Dolores, whose name
means Sadness, will sit by you and thank
any mourners as if each knocked
on her dream-house door and wished

to demonstrate the vacuum,
the beautiful Hoover she bought
in 1948, forever your bride.

• • •

You hung in every game until the sheriff
of Alameda County appeared one morning
in 1957 at 17020 Via Pasatiempo and kicked us
out of the house in the name
of Pacific Finance. Neighbors hung back,
gawking at the shame on the weed-wild lawn
where our tumbled furniture was bright
and wet with dew. What we owned of it
I moved to Grandma's. It was then I noticed
you'd quit coming home. I remember the Frigidaire
slipped off the dolly. I could either
hold it or be crushed. I held it.
I hunted you in whatever bar
I was getting drunk in.
Some nights I'd kill you
playing any game you called, end up
losing my car all over Oakland but
outdrinking you until you begged
forgiveness and told me again
about the great life we all
would have lived if you hadn't turned down
the first Volkswagen dealership west of the Rockies.

• • •

I had a dream at the end of winter.
I never remember my dreams, but Tom,
so ravaged he could hardly walk, came at me,
ripped-up old grease-rags stuffed
in his chest cavity—
came at me and forced me to ride
in his rusted-out 1966 gold
Cadillac Eldorado convertible. I knew
he'd come back to kill us,
but he raised a shotgun to his open mouth
and fired twice and began laughing.
Tom, you fought me, you roared in agony,
Mother grabbed the gun from you,
you fought, I was finally stronger, I
stripped the bathrobe off you. Tom,
in my dream
you weigh eighty pounds.

• • •

You cried into the telephone, "Goddamn,
I don't *feel* malignant!"
"Just skin and bones, not any better
or worse, just less and less," said
her last letter. Your wife is showing
her bridge-club friends the insurance policy—
"Does this say I get ten-thousand dollars?"
I remember your last words to me,
"Don't get cancer."
I said "OK," only that, so never
in my life called you Father or Tom
or Asshole or anything to your face,
and I pulled toward the door, through it
into the San Lorenzo sunshine you'd bought
for eighty-eight down and

eighty-eight a month in 1946, and surely
the sky still trembled, star-hot and beautiful,
but up and down the "Via" all
the little lawns were burning under
the endless, blue-gold California drought.

. . .

Afraid I was too late,
I sent you a letter—"I'm sorry
I'll never see you again. You don't
need to answer this letter." You
didn't answer, and never will—
dead suddenly in a splattery circle
of blood (must have been coughing hard)
on a rented kitchen floor, sprawled
in pajamas, dishwasher hoses pulled off,
racks and clamps and screws all scattered,
the final job of fixing. Then her phone call—
"Honey, it happened," then every detail of how
she felt when she found him, the mess of it,
how Paulie, the youngest, put the dishwasher
back together and cleaned up the blood.
Ah, thank God for Maggie, Avis, and Mabel,
for the Friendship Club and crazy Aunt Netty,
for the Bombshells bowling league, and Betty's
Fun-Tour Bus to Reno, for Mervyn's On The Plaza
where, age sixty, she can still make slots money
clerking part-time in Fabrics.

. . .

When spring returned to Maryland and we opened our win-
dows, I remembered you were still alive. I was appalled. I
saw you weeping in some solid tumor ward. I saw a corpse
kept alive by pain that no one would unplug, and sorrow

finally filled me and pressed hard against my own aging organs, and I wrote that letter with its little lies of *Sorry*. I finally called you by a name, *Tom*, and I meant it—and I kept writing something else, which *was* too late, that ends:

Man, you're living through
to one more summer,
like a thing that will not die.
May the sports get great on TV,
may your pain be brief,
may you not think back on your life,
may the broken-down grease-monkeys of Oakland
bless you.

"THE OPEN DOOR"

My mother's one "original oil,"
frame within frame, skewed the wall
of our basic frame housebox lost

somewhere in the centerless
suburb expanding like the universe
across chest-high tule marshes,

quaking mudflats, rumored quicksand,
and silent reptilian sloughs
sliding toward the Bay, across

crystal red, purple, green
salt basins, overtaking even
the gull-swarmed mountain of the dump

and the shack-town where fat
stupid white girls sat
in rusted cars, giving tit for dimes.

San Lorenzo's dream-molecule—
tiny rooms locked to helix of hall,
houses chained down by linked lawns—

leapt and spread beyond my creek
that once could rage and flood,
a storm-drain now, gravel-gray concrete

plumbing cored under a fresh-poured
freeway erasing the apricot orchard,
beet fields, and rabbit farms

tended by scary brown Portuguese
and Japanese men so old they all
shook like small dead trees,

yelling gibberish at us as
they vanished. The frames, always
misaligned, set my mother's

"colonial maple" dining nook
dustily atilt. "The Open Door"
I named it, a vague watercolor

looking rained-on where I entered
fore-foreground and hovered at
its wooden table, invisible but

there: my tense, magnified head
just off left-canvas, inferred
from a crooked straightback chair.

I looked out through the upper
open half of a door—"Dutch door"
she called it, as if spruce words

made a door severed at the belly,
neither open nor closed, magically
nice, its knife edges hidden

in the milky wash of the brush.
So I sat still and saw what I could,
including what I couldn't: a path

undiminishing, winding down
from the unseen house (I imagined
golden stucco, open window,

a warm poppy breeze), way down
but *up* too, flowing into flight
below green-shadowed hills, beyond

any question of verticality, through
to a valley revealing a river
widening to the sea, a blue

overstaining blue, ending in
ivory mist that allowed no end.
No one but me moved in that scene,

its wispy colors deepened by my eye
the hours and days when I lived
exploring all that pallid country,

following every trackless trail,
climbing over fading pink and yellow
crests to find the sunless other

realm of the canvas, thick with trolls
whispering under iron bridges,
runnels convulsing like black eels—

snake-caves, elves' graves, ogre's midden—
until I was groin-deep, fording slime,
but then a half-ruined woods and a sudden

swirling of mist-light: it was my creek
come back, running clean over the slag
of San Lorenzo, rubble of cracked

toilets, concrete spillage, oddments
of pipe, steel rods, wire, nails,
abandoned windows, doors, with tools

of all kinds dropped as wastage, and more:
its junk-bed shining, the creek was flowing
with every shape of good scrap lumber.

So *here* was my raft—just haul it in—
one day for drying, choosing, fitting,
a second for lashing, hammering, launching,

and I'd be gone. It would take all night,
by stone-fire and toad-glimmer, to touch
the Bay's first tidal outthrust,

but I'd soon be caught, spun seaward, clear—
her house left stranded, a pastel smear
the rising moon would make disappear.

THE MELMAC YEAR

1.

Then it was still called hard rubber,
machined, grainy striations
whorled like giant thumbs, created
I believed in the atom smasher—
the modern homemaker's dinnerware.
Even new, it seemed worn, filmed
with a paleo-plastic dust,
but stronger than iron or stone,
guaranteed to last lifetimes,
another great breakthrough
thanks to World War II.

So my mother kept working
toward her service for twelve,
sixty unbreakable pieces to earn:
amassing stacks of Rinso boxtops
and Philip Morris buy-'em-by-the-carton bonus coupons,
solving (I helped) the acrostics in the Oakland *Tribune*,
winning canasta tourneys and hula-hula contests,
selling jewelry door to door (as I held steady the gaudy
    displays),
and bearing down to get, almost every chance,
the Lucky Frame Gold Pin strike in the Ladies
Monday Dirty Laundry 650 handicap league.

Sometimes she'd make me go in Safeway
for the Melmac demonstrations.
I'd stand at the table, staring at my shoes,
thinking up fake names. I'd change my voice
and ask what I had to ask,

then meet her outside; wait, return—
claiming free prizes until they said don't come back.
Take any color, she told me.
Later she'd try to swap it for blue.

She never missed a Melmac night.
Church bazaars, movie palaces, roller rinks,
bingo emporiums, and peewee golf
grand openings, the long-awaited unveilings
of every latest make and model—
she was there. After dark in 1949
heaven became a spiring city of searchlights,
all looking for her. Any magnesium beam
might guide her to the El Dorado of blazing Melmac.

I don't think I ever knew
that you could simply buy it.

2.

At last my mother completed her set of Melmac.
San Lorenzo was here to stay.
The sycamore twig stuck in front
of each little slab rancher
finally rooted. The Admiral Nimitz Freeway
had launched its slow course south toward us.
Lawns grew tall enough to burn
the straw-brown that we called golden.
No Negroes moved in, or Mexicans,
and no Okies that anybody knew of.
No one but America
could make an atom bomb. And one noon
an Army surplus blimp sagged low
to celebrate the new, still unstriped
Village Parking Plaza, a vastness

of asphalt acres lifting, oozing,
curling at the edges—
so fresh a black
the blimp's shadow
sank beneath the tar.

The wives of San Lorenzo gazed upward.
Bright housedresses pressed against
the county sheriff's rope. The blimp
was idling over the Plaza's center,
more vibration than sound,
more heat than shape. Upon an X
made of shimmering tape stood a man
in a white suit waving pennants.
Suddenly his arms jerked downward
like a stricken dowser. A squadron
of seagulls scrambled. The man ran.
My mother let go my hand, pushed ahead
as the blimp's belly opened and the sky
turned into a crackled, then collapsing
dome of Melmac.

The ropes did not hold—
deputies fled as the wives
rushed to catch the Melmac.
Slices of pink and green and yellow
and my mother's blue
scudded down hard at them.
The cups hit first, thunking heads.
The bowls punched and gouged.
Plates and saucers slapped and cut.
Some women reached up, palms outward
in acceptance or prayer, as if the projectiles
would waft and settle into some perfect

vision of Melmac displayed in the finest homes.
They were the worst bloodied.
Some stumbled out crying,
hair and dresses ruined,
dazedly clutching maybe a cup.
Then my mother emerged, staggering, smiling,
with arms crossed, embracing
at least twenty tar-stained pieces,
looking around for me for help.

The whole three miles home, every house
like our house, my mother's shoes
thwacked off the sidewalk,
leaving black tracks.

3.

So then she had it all, all
blue. High on her special shelf
cups gripped cups,
bowls brimmed tight with bowls,
saucers clicked into saucers, and
the plates—triuned for meat,
potatoes, and carrots or peas—
grasped together like vertebrae.

After the rare meals served upon Melmac,
I was the one who washed the dishes.
Alone at the sink, suds rising, I loved
the simple, solid sense of them.
I wanted thousands more, of every color,
to build towers climbing up
and out of that house.
Soaped, scrubbed, scraped,
scored, scarified, scarred if need be,

but *clean*. Annealed in my care,
they locked, locked, locked
each into the other. Even when my mother
wept behind her bedroom door,
I never knew so sure, so right a fit.

DAVE'S CIRCUS

As soon as school was out the boy worked to build the circus in his backyard. He hacked down weeds and laid out walkways and miniature pavilions, handpainted big ENTER and EXIT signs, cut up blank paper into tickets and on each one printed DAVE'S CIRCUS—10¢. The customers would be channeled from attraction to attraction and spend more money at each.

He had his fat lady lined up and his strong man, a half-dozen clowns, an aerialist (persuaded she could climb a stepladder and walk across a tightened clothesline), a reptile pit (some frogs and a garter snake), a Wild Man of Borneo (on a staked rope), an elephant troupe (large neighborhood dogs were in training), and a den of lions that he himself would tame (the meanest cats were being collected)—and an extra-special feature, the death-defying Man of Steel, who could feel no pain.

He had talked Leroy into being this hero because Leroy was blubbery with a very fat ass, which, the boy figured, would really feel almost no pain—not too much, at least, from the "amazing fearless feat" that he had invented for Leroy. He had invested in a package of darts. Leroy would be bent over, wearing thin pants and no underwear, with his big ass sticking up, exposed to the patrons. The customers would pay a nickel apiece for the darts and from ten feet away try to throw them so they'd stick in Leroy's ass. If a dart stuck, they'd win a worthless prize. He knew he'd make a fortune on this, and he'd give Leroy a cut.

The circus opened with only a few of the attractions operating. The fat lady and strong man showed up and put themselves on inert display. The snake pit was not horrible. The clowns looked clownish but didn't know what to do. The aerialist performed by falling off the clothesline repeatedly. But there was a good crowd, and the Man of Steel was an instant hit. The only thing the circus-goers wanted to do was throw darts at Leroy's ass.

The first ten minutes or so, all the darts bounced off, and Leroy played his part, yelling, "I feel no pain! I'm made of steel!" He had always been cowardly, a schoolyard joke, every bully's favorite victim—a huge, soft weakling who in some way or another was hurt every day. Now he was the Man of Steel. Then a few darts nicked him, not sticking, but the points bit before they fell away. And Leroy stopped yelling, and stiffened. Then a dart stuck. Leroy yelped and shuddered as the boy shouted "Winner!" and quickly pulled out the dart. He awarded the prize (an old comic, a skate key, a doll's head were available on an orange-crate shelf), then sold darts to the next customer. Very soon another dart stuck, and blood showed through the pants. Leroy started whimpering.

He actually took a third dart.

It went in kind of deep. He was heaving up as the boy reached to extract it, and lurched around, his face collapsing in fear and grief and hate, convulsing into sobs. And he ran straight out of the backyard, ignoring the walkways marked by string, with the dart bobbing in his ass.

With Leroy gone, the circus-goers soon departed. A few wanted their money back. They didn't get it, but there would be free admission the next day when, the boy promised, the rest of the attractions would be in full operation even if Leroy couldn't be convinced to return.

And the boy immediately started to work. He would somehow really tighten and brace the highwire, tie those big dogs in a line and get them all to beg at once, make the clowns do something funny, and talk the ugly retarded kid into being the Wild Man. And there was still a lot of construction to finish. So he worked and worked and didn't stop until the hacksaw, something he had never used before, jumped out of its groove in the iron pipe he was cutting into bars for the lions' cage, and with the full thrust of the blade underway, it went into and almost through the bone high in his left index finger. When he found his mother she screamed and, as soon as she could find a neighbor who could drive, rushed him to the doctor. The finger took so many stitches it was virtually sewn back on.

The circus closed. The attractions soon disappeared in the returning overgrowth of weeds. And Leroy, who would later join the Highway Patrol, marry beauty, and open a successful Foster's Freeze, called the boy his enemy for life.

CLOTHES PILE

Now and then my mother
would dump some clean laundry
on her bedroom floor and for days
my little brothers and I would root around
in the Clothes Pile, as she called it, to find
pants, socks, shirts, underwear.
John and Paul, close in size, had to fight.
The Clothes Pile would steadily shrink away
until we couldn't find it. Still she'd shout,
"Look in the Clothes Pile!" So then
we'd have to pick through the Dirty Clothes
to get the least smelly socks, the least
shit-streaked shorts—about which time
my mother would do the Wash. The foaming Bendix
spilled across the garage floor,
and finally I'd help "hang the Wash."
A new Clothes Pile appeared for the taking.

My best friend, Bobby, lived without
a Clothes Pile. His house was just like ours
except turned around. He had clean clothes
hung in his closet, folded in drawers.
Blue water rose in his toilet bowl.
His father was a graduate of Brigham Young University,
an accountant for the federal government,
a lieutenant commander in the Naval Reserve,
and received *True* and *Argosy* magazines.
He bought a new Buick every three years.
All my friends' fathers had jobs.
Bobby and I found an open box
of Sheiks in his father's nightstand;
opened one to measure full size.

His mother usually asked me to stay
for dinner: roast beef so bloody
I was afraid it was alive; trout
swimming off the bones. Desserts invented
by a high-speed blender. All cornucopian,
a word I knew the meaning of
in 8th grade when I knew the meaning
of every word, until my teacher, tired
by my goading ("Ask me any word, ask me *any* word,
go on, ask me"), asked me "puerile" and "fatuous."
But I had finally been adopted, my dream.
I bent close, breathing in the steam
of green beans, broccoli, carrots, peas,
all running with liquid butter.

Bobby's mother cleared the table
directly after dinner and washed the dishes.
I fell in love with the wall-to-wall rug
I lay upon and pressed my belly and groin into,
shoes off, feet in the air, gazing
into the flawless TV: *Maverick*, *Lawman*,
Tales of Wells Fargo, and always the Wednesday
Night Fights—Dick Tiger, Bobo Olsen, Joey Giardello,
Joey Giambra, Gene Fullmer, Ralph "Tiger" Jones
in the middleweight division alone. Watching
until it got too late to go home
and Bobby's mother asked if I'd like
to sleep over.
                    I fell in love
with Bobby's closets and drawers,
how he was always so clean,
almost as strong as me, good-smelling,
his body blond and downy while mine
was becoming the hairy thing I heard

40

made girls sick. And I fell in love
with the cold sheets on Bobby's bed.
I loved to trace their hard creases
with my toes and let my bare legs slide
over to touch his legs as the bed warmed
and my arm wavered and fell across his chest
whenever I got to sleep over with Bobby at age fourteen.

THE OLD HOG FARM

Pinhole eyes burn white, caught
in the yellow reach of his flashlight—
then, squeals pitching higher, their fine
sandpapery scrape of nails clawing
toward him, down the rotten tin chute
where pig guts once quivered and slid.

Frozen prone, he's a hard skinny line
locking in the muzzle of his new .22.
The earth that holds him is solid, shaky
hogshit, offal, hogbrains, blood—
a century of slaughter turned under
and compacted a hundred strata deep.

But skulls can sometimes break
the crust, and glow above the muck.
He's seen one. It went in his sack, small
collection slowing the advance
of lawns, patios, mothers, dogs, morning
across his snake-rich, rat-rich tidal flats.

He doesn't have much time—
owls and bats already gone,
the hills behind Hayward just silvering,
and the wiry little cries now shrilling,
closing fast. He sights up a tunnel
of endless stench, and starts shooting.

LOVE LIFE

The first hair that showed
above his mouth
he let grow. Others soon appeared.
He didn't know what to do with them.

But a hat, a stained,
bent fedora, hid his eyes
and shadowed his general
beardlessness, adding years.

Then the mustache formed,
soft as cilia, and framed
the King Edward cigars he puffed,
inhaling, aging him more.

He buttoned the collar button
of his white shirt
and filled out his shoulders
with a tan sport coat.

His pants, belt, shoes
didn't appear in the mirror,
so he didn't care about those.
He was big enough in any case,

man enough then to fool all
the bartenders on East 14th,
the longest street in Oakland,
ordering Scotch or rye, "water back."

He liked the old men's bars,
men his father's age. They
sat next to him and asked
if he played football and how

his love life was, told him
dirty jokes, gave him cigarettes.
He looked powerful and dark in the mirror.
His friends bought him drink after drink.

THE THING

The night we saw *The Thing*
twice—popcorn, jujubes
gumming and grouting teeth—
turned black as a bat's wing,

black slogging our walk home
as if each step grew instant
roots, left twisted plants
feeding in the asphalt loam

of our rich fears for blocks
back. 1952—
no way to know then who
or why we were: our cocks

caught in continual change,
red bean to meat to spindrift,
all matter whipped in shape-shift,
no limit to the strange

aromas, hairiness, shames
enfolding us, and yes,
an earth-green joy unguessed,
like our secret real names,

the Never Knowns. All flowed,
sprang, melted, danced, wound
around a downy bone—
and *that* much we could hold,

that only were we sure of.
So no great shocks or horrors
when lawn-deer, birdbaths, porch chairs
shook, bled, began to move,

seeming just the further surge
of an eight-foot stalk of wild
male vegetable, "killed"
by puny humans' voltage—

but ha! Rising, he roared
toward idiot manflesh ("Science"
appealing then to "Conscience"—
the fools!). Ropy tendrils powered

by rage tore men apart.
Then sped he to his pods,
his frozen little gods;
thawed each ensheathèd heart,

stroking their pulse alive
upon a finer principle
than red, viscous *animal*—
his ice-cave clean of such love

as drove us nigh the pit
of curses, hisses, howls
to glimpse one flash of the whole
white mystery: bare tit.

No, when all the uniform
suburban junk that night
convulsed and crawled upright,
we felt some arctic fog-storm

swirl up and pour hot, sweet
juice into dry fixities,
pump ichor-sap, grow *knees*
upon the dead Dead of the street,

tilting them like the planet
toward us, with lurching strides
of new *things* seeking . . . brides?
Fade. Then: THE END—OR IS IT?

Tricks of moon-shadow perhaps,
but we'd seen what we saw
way deep, before—in the raw
mewling of our infant naps?—

so with no hesitation,
no cause to cry alarums
(dull villagers outslept charms),
we dug hallucination

for the first time. Oh, soon came
It, Them, The Fly, then *And
God Created Woman*—damned,
our pods swelled, split. Aflame,

we smoked through triple features,
our brains no more than sun-
thick grubs, ripening again
and again to feed our creatures.

THE BAIT

I was the bait, sixteen. The plan
was I'd sit on a bench in Union Square
at midnight when they came out.
When one that looked rich enough
cruised by, I'd let my thighs
relax apart and flex my ass.
He'd stop, hold up an unlit cigarette,
then sit next to me and ask
for a light. Very soon he would be
asking me if I had a girlfriend,
if she did things to me I liked.
That's when I'd know—especially
if he glanced down at my display
of crotch and said, "I'll bet
you got a big one there, big enough
to make any girl happy"—I'd know
for sure I had one hooked. I was
supposed to let him press his leg
against mine, let him reach
his arm along the back of the bench
and stroke my neck, wait for him
to say, "You seem like a friendly boy.
I really like friendly boys.
Do you feel friendly tonight?"
The idea was I'd get him so hot
that when I finally said, "How about
the men's room in the Shell down on Geary?"
he'd go with me, anticipating nothing
but my dick. When we got there, I'd let him
get on his knees and unzip me, even
have it out for a second so he'd
deserve what he was about to get. Then

my friends would rush out of the toilet
and we'd all beat the shit out of him,
take his money and watch, take his
pants and shoes, and run out and dive
into the revving car. *That*
was the plan.
                What happened was this
smelly man I never saw coming
sat down next to me. I did give him
a light, and inside that little glow
I saw his stained, hairy fingers
trembling the cigarette, and his face
beaten like one of our fathers
sneaking in, bruised with booze—
except the man's eyes
looked straight into mine.
He said, "You want a blowjob?"
I was startled and offended.
I was supposed to get seduced.
I wanted some smooth talking,
some intelligent, evil style.
What made him think he could just *ask*?
"No thanks," I said, sitting there
bulging in my tight chinos, shivering
in my thin lime-green shirt chosen
to show off my new muscles.
We sat silent a couple of minutes.
I saw he was looking toward Powell Street
and had spotted our lookout. Then
the man gripped my knee, hard.
He said, "You *are* really cute.
Whenever you do want a good blowjob,
just come back by yourself."
Now that I liked. That was tender.

That made the whole fucked-up plan
worth it. He got up, and before
he walked too far away to hear,
I said "Thank you." My knee
felt warm. For days, it tingled warm,
as if he had damaged some nerve.

FIRST HIGH

Harold Hatakeda's father owned
the tire shop, corrugated tin lean-to
like shelter thrown up after a bomb blast,
doorless, but secured at night
by father or son always sleeping there.
Mr. Hatakeda was shorter even
than Harold, his skin creased, vulcanized
dark yellow, deep-grainy like worn stone.
We made sure not to see him on Harold's shift.
We hung out with Harold—his skin smooth
hard caramel—usually in the re-cap room
where slabs of rubber heated to the point
they'd melt and bond. Two huge doughnut molds
banged, heaved, seethed against bolts loosening
in the concrete floor, erupting black magma
but somehow never actually exploding.

Bob and Frank and Harold talked a lot
about cars (I listened, said *yeah, man*)—John Diaz
on a midnight mountain road, way north of Redding,
a logging truck swung across the line,
killed him, and *totalled* his loaded, cherried-out Fury.

We are as close to death as we've ever been.
Harold's rolled the reefer; I've got the match.
We hope we don't end up complete addicts
like Sinatra in *The Man with the Golden Arm*,
though to be warmed that way by Kim Novak
would not be terrible. The county sheriff,
the school nurse, and a priest have told us
if we take one puff we *will* get hooked,
and we believe them. But the radio's tuned

to Jumpin' George—an Earl Bostic number,
then Lloyd Price, Al Hibbler, Cozy Cole,
Shirley & Lee, Guitar Slim, Brother Ray—
it's *Sepia Serenade*. We know how Negroes
love smoking marijuana, and so will we.
We got it from a Negro in West Oakland.
Harold knows jujitsu. Ten years ago
the A-bomb dropped. Harold lights the reefer,
drags his eyeballs out; then it fires up,
and he coughs a dense cloud, now waits, puffs,
inhales warily, holds it in. "It's not
a cigarette," he croaks, and passes it.
So this is what we do. We take turns
sucking in the smoke. Who holds it longest? Me.

We laugh. Watch the rubber bubble. "How
you feel, man?" "Fucking great, man." Laugh.
I hope I haven't turned into a hophead dope fiend.
They're wondering how fast John Diaz was going—
ninety at least, that was Johnny, downhill
when the fucking truck sliced the Fury's top off.
Frank is wondering if they saved the engine,
could he get it and drop it in his Merc,
and John Diaz would sort of live on that way. . . .

I drift over by the hydraulic hoist,
then wander out unmissed. Cars whooshing by
inside some tremendous breathing, suddenly cold,
sun gone without a sound, headlights cool
and glowing past my invisibility.
I really hope the cops don't take me in.
I don't want to kick cold turkey in Santa Rita,
because all the cars immaculately cruising
Paseo Grande and every girlfriend in them

are mine, and I got nickels bulging my pocket
and I'm walking toward the bowling alley,
shoulders, hips, head all boppin'
to the rhythm of pinballs that never tilt.

"Honey Hush" - Joe Turner, 1953

1.

"Turn off them waterworks, baby—
they don't move me no more." Good shout
to shut up weepy mothers, pissed-off girls.
Today that jukebox exhumed from Village Bowl
would cost a lifetime setting pins.
Who can excavate those ten shining lanes,
striations of hardwoods oiled golden,
and exquisitely, with razor and acid, strip
the dross off that frieze of pompadoured boys
suspended between pinballs and the jukebox
always flowing down over itself
but never changing its ice-cream colors
cast in solid light? We're still down there,
in the dim basement bowling alley beneath
the first supermarket in San Lorenzo.

Come down the stairwell, escape the glare
of empty blue California sky. Breath
relaxes, shoulders assume the muscled slope
of adolescent first growth, eyes adjust by
picking out your friends' glow-in-the-dark
lemon-lime and chartreuse flamingo'd nylon
peggers, or the bleached white T-shirts
that barely reach the skinny suede belt
of the low-hung black tight chinos.
Pinball exertions and juke-side boppin'
pulled the shirts out, and hard-guys always left
their ass-cracks and climbing pubic belly-hairs
exposed, hoping maybe some new girls
would come down and replace the skaggy

gum-snappers who cringed just out of reach
with their cherry Cokes and mystery talk.

But no nice kids ever came down to the Village Bowl.
And even the dumb ones—like Eddie Mowbray whose
self-inflicted tattoo never healed, oozed
like a suppurating rose for a year with his sleeve
rolled up, knotted at the shoulder with a pack
of Camels he never removed while bumming smokes
from all of us—even dumb Eddie figured out
why we were the only ones there.
It was because we were there.

2.

Robbie the Pinboy was a slim fifty.
"I'm nothin' but a pin-goof," Robbie said.
"But pin-goofin's great. It's the only job
you can drink beer on all night."

Robbie was a beero—his term. He talked, we listened.
"Boys, a beero's gonna work all day,
work all night for you—just give him his beer.
He sweats it out and gets stronger.
Now a fuckin' wino'll puke his guts up,
couldn't set pins for a blind cripples league.
Winos come down here, think to pin-goof some quick
    money—
they find out." Robbie drank two six-packs
of Lucky Lager during a two-league night,
and drank a six-pack before, and always
had a few after, and had drunk a six-pack
that morning and at least another in between.
I never saw him eat more than potato chips.

I liked to set pins on the pair next to Robbie.
I'd watch his moves—the smooth
right-handed sweep across the pit-floor
while scooping up the bowling ball in
the left hand and curling it down the return,
all one motion, then yanking the motor-cord to start
the pinrack rocking downward.
The rack lowered: Robbie's right hand dealt
three pins into the slots, then somehow had more,
sliding pins off his arms and shoulders while
the left hand came up full also
and flipped the last pins in perfectly as
the clanking rack bottomed out and reset
the ivory, red-crowned bulbous Brunswick Kings
into the next quivering triangle.

Never out of breath, Robbie pulled leisurely
at his Lucky Lager as if he had all day
to savor the hops instead of the three to five seconds
before the pins crashed in his other pit.
Behind him, the empty bottles stacked up neatly
like a growth of amber crystal.

I imitated Robbie's technique,
the no-wasted-moves moves, unhurried,
superior to the last instant, then swinging
my legs up and out of the way of the flying pins.
Sometimes I'd get hit. Sometimes I'd coolly toss
a pin *over* the rack and have to go crawling
halfway up the alley after it, smearing myself
with sweaty oil, while the bowlers applauded,
throwing pennies down the gutters. These things
never happened to Robbie, but then he didn't
take the chances I did, but then
he never had to.

"Fuck them, Dave," Robbie yelled to me.
"Bowlers are fuckin' assholes.
You're fine, a real pin-goof."

3.

After pinsetting, flush with five-dollar bills,
we'd go riding in somebody's car,
hair greasy in the wind,
salt cooling on our foreheads and shirts.
We'd pool our money and pay for the beer—
Robbie would buy it. In the back of the car
he was suddenly so old, a shrunken wisp,
stick-armed, hollow-chested, wheezy,
taking up no room, not even there, or
spraying us with affectionate spittle,
a lot like our fathers. Drinking steadily,
quietly, we'd drift into midnight, deep into
the Hayward Hills. Never any cops
in the Hayward Hills. There we saw
all the stars we ever were to see,
where talk was as precise as it would ever be,
since we knew so few things to talk about,
avoiding all topics of *why* and *because*,
sticking to *who* and *what*, careful about *when*.
There I learned every word inside
a minuscule dictionary,
just driving really in the radio's thick
molasses jive of the DJ between luscious
sets of Johnny Ace, Tiny Bradshaw, Bobby Blue Bland,
Earl Bostic, Ray Charles, Lightnin' Hopkins,
the Penguins. And Big Joe Turner shouting,
"This big black sucker
don't want no talkin' back,
Honey hush!"

"PACHUCO HOP" – CHUCK HIGGINS, 1954

1.

That music puts you in the mood to move,
to stomp some dudes,
to close knuckles around a roll of dimes
and flatten windpipes.
We called our shoes stompers,
whatever style:
crazed brown alligator wingtips,
purple suede, oxblood moccasins,
black dagger-toes, 'sickle boots.
All had horseshoes,
nailheads filed to a point,
steel moonslice taps
studding the soles.
We slipped and slid
on the scored floor
of our underground bowling alley,
dancing on our weapons.
Cut 'em up, blind them,
stomp their balls,
stomp their faces—
gasping chants as we jerked
and skated to the saxophone's
honks and squeals,
Chuck Higgins' instrumental
melodic as fuck-grunts,
no need for words
when your fists could sing.
Do the Dirty Bop—
black chinos hang

from the root of your dick.
More nickels in the jukebox
until Ingah the Skag leads you
into the poolroom's darkest corner
and dry-humps you raw
against your belt buckle,
moaning into your greasy hair
how much she loves only you
and your French kissing,
and you *do* love her
right up to that instant
you groan and are suddenly sticky
and stained and so sore
it'll be two hours before
you can whip it again.
Over your head, in the sun,
the lames are working their bagboy jobs,
wearing white Safeway shirts,
Daddies' bowties,
saying Thank You, opening
bank accounts, going steady,
keeping their flattops waxed,
their shoes always soft
and powdery white.

2.

Then we rose
from the Village Bowl,
scouted the vast parking plaza
for unlocked cars,
a bottle of bourbon in the backseat,
an easy hotwire up front.
Mostly we snuck into the Lorenzo Theatre
to catch the end of A-Bomb

monster movies—a buck to whoever
got bare tit first.
No one would win
unless Ingah was there alone,
then we all won. The main feature
was Intermission, the candy counter
where always stood Bobo (no
last name), Bobo in everybody's way
but no one complaining,
his force-field radiating
off coconut biceps,
off his back muscles straining
the green parrots perched
in the tree of his silk *kanaka* shirt,
heavy red vines twisting to snakes
that spelled out KOREA—
Bobo who was too bad for the CYA
and showed no fear in Folsom,
the King of Intermission.
Once in the Lorenzo Theatre
Bobo shouted to me, "Hey Dave,
man, fucker, what's happ'nin'?"
Sick with dread, I said enough
to stay alive. And the small fast ones—
Greg Jimenez, Junior Pacheco,
Candy Candalerio, Juano Ramos—
the fine-boned pretty ones
with delicate knives, whose speech
would flash to Spanish
like the songs of copper birds,
they all got me high and whispered
"Hey Dave, man, fucker,
you oughta be *pachuco*," then laughed
their girlish, private crack-up.

Big joke, but why not?
They let me hang around—
at sixteen I was 5' 10", 180,
a pinsetter since I was twelve,
stacking the heavy wood every night,
and they saw, too, that I'd be
as crazy as they wanted,
both drunk and cool, indifferent
to bluffs, poses, jive, feints,
always ready with my stompers,
assuming my Marciano crouch,
touch me and you're dead, fucker.
An easy choice—I'd be *pachuco.*

3.

All I had to do
was carve a cross, a
cuneiform crucifix,
in the meat that bulged
between my thumb and first finger,
gouge a few sun-rays toward the wrist.
Best to use
a red-hot razorblade
and immediately pour blue-black ink
into the welling blood and let
infection do its work—
easy. Then in secret
lift the bandage, show off
the festering brand, let Ingah
and the white guys gaze
upon my inflamed *pachuco* ankh.
But it didn't take—it healed
purple, then pink, then me,
not even a scar.

Did I cut deep enough?
Did I even do it?
I never was *pachuco*,
and all the toughness
was only delirious fear.
And Chuck Higgins himself
was about as bad as Louis Prima
or Vido Musso, both fat old
horn-blowers who, years later,
I challenged to fights in
Tahoe showbars where they were faking
R&B—boozy rhinestone stiffs,
ruffles, coal-black wigs, toad-sized
pinky rings, snakeskin elevator
boots with chrome zippers, deader
than the droning slot machines—
and got myself neatly thrown out,
punched sober by a pro
who knew how not to hurt his hands.

4.

But Chuck knew
the stomper's beat—
bony fists, deadly feet
fighting their own shadows cast
by low, dim-fluorescent, glow-
in-the-dark rhythms, pumping out
style and legend, like Bobo
cleaning up five cops,
the entire football team,
stomping all our fathers,
all myth and dream except a few
real scuffles that mixed tears
with snot with blood

and maybe broke some metatarsals
and teeth but never cost
anybody's eyes or balls.
All that ended when, stoned
on nothing stronger than testosterone,
I woke up in Juvenile Hall—
seventy-two hours in solitary
to see if I had a contagion,
then I joined the Population.
My best cellmate in Juvie,
Roderigo, was my age, seventeen.
I read to him, and he lit
our contraband cigarettes
on wires in the electric switch.
He got out before me.
He was gonna make big money
lumping on the Oakland truck docks.
I stayed in long enough
to hear the counselor one day
announce to all us assembled
hard-guys, mean dudes, *pachucos*,
ugly motherfuckers, black skulls,
Satan's Slaves, Born-to-Kill-tattooed
mad-dog stomp artists, all us
miserable, lonely, terrified,
tears-in-the-pillow, loveless jack-offs,
that Roderigo had been shot to death
in a liquor store holdup.
"Let that be a lesson to you,
you assholes," the man said.

CHERRY

for Joe Cardarelli

chopped channeled raked
molded lowered louvered—
teenage lungs breathing
fiberglass dust
epoxy fumes
nicotine
        frenching
headlights past midnight
in a closed secret shed
muscle-power sanders ceaselessly smoothing
Sepia Serenade on KSAN mingling Johnny Ace
with solemn boys' voices appraising
contour texture slope bevel beauty
how to shape the next 'glass sheet
layering its sticky sheen just right
to catch the ineffable curve
and shame the world's ugliness away—
how to hold and harden perfection
under the heat lamp clamped close
and left to burn inches above it all night
risking ruinous hissing bubbles
but nothing sang that didn't croon destruction

so five-grand worth at least
of real '50s cash
hundreds of hours out of our timeless lives
so that we could lounge way back
on fleshy Tijuana Naugahyde
upholstered by the Hollywood muffler's throbbing
through handleless lockless cardoors clicked

open by magical solenoids hidden under fenders
shaded eyes even
with the planes of rolled-down windows
sightless behind the hood cowling where
the supercharger seethed
smoke rings holding as we cruised East 14th's
five murmurous miles between Van's Deluxe
Drive-In and the first A&W in the Eastbay

revving the hidden engine seductively
other engines responding with quick
questioning growls hinting infinite potency
expert tilting of Lucky Lager quart bottles
warm rich foaming swigs invisible to cops
drinking steady mellowlike
so cool with car radio low singing
Earth Angel
               in command of everything
in the world except our imperious
impervious hard-ons those other loaded engines
keeping us cruising looking long
and long for girls in Daddies' cars
sing-songing our polished-to-perfection invitations
hey beautiful you and your beautiful
friend lookin for a party we're goin
to a great party can you find a coupla
more girls wanna come we got beer

this again and again a hundred times a night
through year-long California summers
until one or two A.M. and the gleaming *paseo* thinning out
cars heading to Seven Hills Road in Livermore
for the real drag racing or out
to the bottomless flooded quarry or the stripped

65

apricot orchard or the ghostly abandoned hog farm
in search of rumored rumbles with *pachucos*
or off to actual parties we never found
and never a glance never a reply
except insulting from the girls
just as we wanted
never anything to disturb or stain or blur
or awaken our perfection

MARGE BARNES

More than forty years have passed and I'm still not sure I'm
    safe
to tell about Marge Barnes a woman really old to us way into
    her twenties
who ended up a quarter mile down an apricot orchard road
    with us after midnight
rotten fallen apricots squished oozy under my shoes like soft
    fat bugs
mixing in the black air with all the other excreta rising from
    the fertilized earth
and Marge Barnes saying *you said you'd take me to the San
    Jose Greyhound*
and we saying *we will after you do it why don't you just do
    it?*
wondering what did she care she was so old and beat-up
    scrawny-looking hitchhiking on dark Highway 17 south
    of deserted Alvarado shit we were doing her a favor and
    gave her some of our beer besides
and she saying *I've never done five guys at one time before*
and we saying *we won't do it hard*
and she saying *well OK then*
moth-streaked moonlight and cigarette lighters glimpsing
    five boys pants open fully exposed stroking themselves
    more for each others' eyes than for hers
both doors of the '50 Ford open someone has to go first
    where she lay waiting across the carseat
low whistles and encouraging grunts for him (probably Phil
    the oldest seventeen who said he had done it before)
appalling mysterious struggling jerks like a trapped animal
    in the dimming interior light
my turn next-to-last and I *was* easy not even knowing where
    it was in the thick slick juice tangled down there

but something did feel like enough to finish me in ten
    seconds
so I don't know if that really counted as my first time
Marge Barnes just saying *you're nice how many more?*
but now comes the crime
we backed out to 17 drove a ways pulled over all in
    agreement without saying a word and told her to get out
and she did saying *that's not fair I thought you were good
    boys*
but we left her standing there the highway emptier than ever
    a warm night at least
and we howled down the highway to San Jose not because
    we had any idea of what to do in San Jose
except we still had beer and that was where we'd lied to
    Marge Barnes we were going.

TIJUANA

The first thing you wanted to see was the girl
who fucked a donkey on stage, picked quarters
out of your teeth with her cunt, the girl
whose nether lips smiled as the drunk
gringo drummer ground it out.
                              Marine, you're seventeen,
you can drink twenty Carta Blancas and still get hard
for the whore at the end of the crazy cab ride.
How sweet she was, whispering, "Are you in?
Are you done?" They let you back over the border
when you remembered your name.

THROUGH THE WALL

1.

Dirty, rotten, filthy, stinking, stupid
drunk he was, staggering, slobbering,
cursing every night, coming home at last
resort to the wife, child, life he
hated, the little tract rancher he hated
(despairing neighbors mowed its front lawn
while the backyard, hidden by fences, grew
to where kids from all over paid me
a nickel for the "guided jungle tour,"
my first money-making scheme ever).

Lurching through the flimsy front door,
staring about like a creature escaped,
he'd attack the first "nice" thing he saw—
ripping apart my mother's hula-hula skirt,
melting under the broiler the Tupperware
she sold at parties, tearing to shreds
the Van Gogh reproductions she'd ordered
for the dining nook, and hurling to the floor
the cold, tragic supper she always left for him.
Then he'd go after her, and then
I could no longer fight waking up.
The crashing and screaming I could weave
into my dream, but at her first weeping
I bolted almost awake and shivered and
swore in the dark until her crying pitched
higher and the smacks sounded too solid
and I'd get up and walk, resigned,
a sleepy boy doing his chores,
down the short hallway
to stop him.

Nothing heroic—
I'd just stand in the door of their bedroom
where it usually got to, and stare at him,
my mother cowering, her face melting with tears,
hair frantic, nightgown off her shoulders, indecent,
and she'd see me and moan "Oh, Honey!"
as if no one had ever known
sorrow before, as if she'd discovered
a new realm of motherly emotion and was
trembling to try it on me. And then he'd turn,
abruptly, as if I'd roped him or waved
a rodeo clown's cape, and he'd focus on me,
like *Who's this kid?* and say, so soberlike,
measured: "C'mere, you son-of-a-bitch bastard,
and I'll throw you through the wall."

But then it was enough only to stand
where I was, my mother wading toward me as he
toppled onto the bed, repeating his promise,
mumbling that secret between us, until his
snoring started and I'd fight out of her
hugs or clutchings and get back to my room
to lie awake imagining what it would be like
to be thrown through the wall.

2.

Would the wall give easily? Maybe so. I was a hard item,
and if I balled myself up, maybe I'd just penetrate the wall
like a big bullet and land, still hard, on the other side (in the
"laundry room" that would be, a dank closet in which a pile
called the Dirty Clothes was always rising). He was that
strong; he could just put me through that wall faster than I
would be hurt. Or maybe there would be some resistance—it
was a wall—and on impact my own power multiplied by his

thrust would just muscle that wall apart in an explosion of plaster, and I'd be dazed, covered with dust, maybe some blood, sprawled on a heap of rubble, but *through the wall* and in one piece. Would he come and lift me up then, both of us laughing?

Or what I really felt would happen—I would be thrown so powerfully that I would warp into another dimension where my body would become an invisible atomic surge and just flow between and through the molecules of the wall, maybe just keep on flowing and resume corporeal shape far from that house, maybe on Mars, where an ancient and noble race of wonderfully intelligent and kind beings lived gracious lives in beautiful cities far below their cool red canals.

I never found out. The summer I was sixteen I was suddenly 5' 10", and 180, and had been perfecting my Marciano weave and uppercut-hook (I could bring it from the floor, every fiber of me from my toes on up propelling that punch) against fearless mirrors and miserable friends who weren't coming around as often as usual. And one night he said, "C'mere, you fucking son-of-a-bitch bastard, and I'll throw you through the wall." And I went.

3.

He was taller than me, his arms bruised,
veiny and corded, his hands huge and
black with impervious grease from a life
of wrestling engine blocks. He looked down at me
with ugly hatred and some surprise,
then joyous contempt. "You fuck . . ." he began,
just as my mother moaned "Oh, David . . ." but made
no move to intervene, and I let loose
the hook. It was absolutely the most
powerful left hook ever thrown.
It was going to catch his right cheekbone high,

exactly where the jaw anchors to the skull,
and crush the ear and temple as well.
I instantly projected in my mind's eye
a slow-motion movie of the blow, complete
with a follow-up short right cross for aesthetics.
He was already a classic still photo capturing
the destructive force of a full heavyweight's hook
landing on target. But he was swaying,
and his head wobbled back just as
my fist reached his jaw—and missed it.

But the punch did land, beautifully,
flush against the wall. They made real walls
in the '50s, even in $6,000 tract houses.
And it *was* a perfect hook. My left arm went
instantly numb up to my shoulder and hung dead.
I was defenseless, but he just continued
his backward lean until he fell on the bed.
He stared at me, shocked, murderous, but once
he hit that bed, he stayed there.
Had I knocked him down with the air mass
condensed in front of my fist?
Could be, because fresh in the wall, head-high,
shone a pristine imprint
of a young human male fist,
a fine, immaculate specimen,
like the first murder fossilized.
It was there I left my unflawed form.
As for my actual hand, the outer knuckles
had simply vanished. It had shifted, canted
about a half-inch back toward the wrist
where a jagged ridge of some strange
new bone stretched the skin,
until it was consumed within

a swelling black and purple hive.
My mother kept crooning
"Oh, David," like a doll.

4.

I walked the streets all night—a beautiful San Lorenzo night:
stars, silence, peacefully sleeping little houses, crisp, cool
wind off the bay, foghorns and train whistles from ten miles
away through the clear darkness. My right hand carried my
left, cradling it against my heart like a killed bird. I knew it
was broken, all wrong, and my wrist, too, was spoiled,
crunched, and even my elbow was bad, making startling,
loud ratchety sounds when feeling came back to it and I tried
moving it a little. I whimpered as I walked, but only out of
physical necessity, not grief, because for some reason I was
happy. I slept a little bit in a parked car, drowsing mostly, or
maybe passing out, fighting the pain for sleep.

I didn't go to a doctor; didn't know how. I wrapped up
the hand and said it was all right. Eventually the hand and
wrist mended—misshapen, but they worked OK and didn't
hurt. A boy's body grants some generous tolerances.

5.

The incident was never mentioned in that house, never al-
luded to. But I know that every day they unavoidably saw
that imprint of a fist in the wall—a clear quarter-inch deep,
not even dusty at the edges, but cleanly compressed. They
had to see it the first thing getting up. And I occasionally
snuck a look at it. The fist became part of the decor, like a
singular piece of naive folk art. I have wondered what the
people who took over our house thought of it. (Two or three
years after that night, we "lost" the house. He quit making
the $88.88-per-month payments, and we were evicted, clas-

sic furniture-on-the-lawn style. But I was pretty much gone anyway.) I imagine the new owners' gasping double-takes at that strange impression six feet up the bedroom wall. "Honey, is that . . . can it be . . . does that look like . . . a fist?" I hope it remains in the wall today. It was perfect of its kind, indeed platonic fistness shadowed forth. I hope it has acquired mystery and legend passed down through the decades of dwellers gazing at it in wonder.

6.

I forgave my father
just about everything,
or did not forgive
but basically decided
not to give a fuck.
That took many years
and many more self-inflicted injuries.
I have spit up their stories
like wormy blood.
And his dying helped.
But one thing is not forgiven—
his only betrayal,
his only real failure
as far as I cared.
I blame him for
letting me,
making me,
try it alone—for never
actually throwing me
through the wall. Now that
would have been something!

17020 VIA PASATIEMPO

How such a little box could hold
sly fifths of I.W. Harper,
one mange-bald mutt, a ten-year-old
tapping the walls for exits—add
great slabs of emptiness like stone,
ashes hardened by his mother's
tears—contain such debris of lives
crowding his head, and kid brothers
no less, love not letting him alone:

I cannot grasp now. Forty years
of faked deaths gone (pick one: eighteen,
drunk, bopping on a roof-edge, beers
swinging both hands, blacked-out, he fell,
four stories up, *back* onto the roof—
so friends, when he came to, told him),
and I'm parked again at the curb,
outstaring that house, stucco scrim
wavery in the sun, demanding proof,

beyond treacherous, fitful cock-
memory, I didn't just *occur*
as randomly as the wild rock-
garden now litters the gone lawn—
bleached gravel bed for castles, elves,
windmills, burros, pagodas, gnomes.
All refract in the plastic sphere
atop mystic cone, swirling selves
into the froth of fragmented poems.

So I wait, if ghosts can meet, for
the asthmatic shade of a boy,

"smart for his age," through the bent door
(creaking slow, gothically as hell)
to escape and enter me. Scare
strange neighbors peeking through their blinds—
I'm the spectre now, heavy, gray
rental-car lurker. Nothing binds
me here, except—worn-out, bland—terror.

LAST SCRAPINGS

1.

Back at it, job I've quit
so many times it must be mine,
breaking strata of petrified oil
off the workfloor of the Arrow Garage.

Old now in this labor,
yet still on my knees, bowing
over the annealed depth of grease,
with scraper and hammer driving
against the slag of his life
since he hired me that summer
more than forty years gone, to find
the floor of his failing shop.

Up to me, of all creatures, to expose
the white concrete of his dream—
he'd keep those pre-war junkers running
and drive a Cadillac painted *Tommy*.
Now, with the floor scraped clean
and swabbed with kerosene,
he'll maybe sell the dump
for a couple of bucks before it's lost.
I get five dollars a day; never paid,
but the calendar's still counting.

So I wedge in, lever down, working
this crack in the crust,
half-grown muscles tearing,
forcing the wide blade deeper under,
until my black tectonics pries free

a heavy plate of sludge-stone,
and all its layers rise
unbroken for my inspection—
shearings and shavings of steel,
detritus of mis-machined pistons,
valves, cams, cylinders, rods;
grindings, scorings, minuscule
razory curlings of steel—
glinting in a thick cross-section
revealing the epoch called Bad Mechanic.

2.

On drunk or hungover days,
dust-yellow blinds close
around his cubbyhole office,
rusted BACK AT pointer stuck at 12—
noon or midnight no matter
because it's never time in the Alcazar Lounge
across the street next to the most forlorn
miniature golf course in Oakland (rain-
rotted carpets, weeds sticking up
from the holes). The men at the bar
keep laughing even when a wife
stands in the barroom door, a little
wailing brother hanging from each hand,
she screaming at him to stop drinking
up the grocery money, and he throws
his change off the bar at her, cursing.

Not opening the shop at all some weeks,
avoiding his "assistant," the retarded
Sid Sidowski, hoping he'll forget
his back pay (which he does), and forgetting
the money owed *him* (a clump of old invoices

spiked on the littered desk, and the nail
still long enough to reach his heart or lungs),
not answering the phone even if it's
Peterbilt calling ten years after
their promise of all the West Coast work
rebuilding their forklift engines (*fucking*
niggerloving jew bastards), and just not doing
the few jobs left but pouring in
some gunk, waiting two weeks, displaying
the usual box of broken parts and
charging for an overhaul, praising
another rescue by his treasured
boring bar that actually wobbles off
whole sixteenths instead of thousandths.

3.

But now I'm getting down close
to bonded sand and gravel, chipping mortar,
scratching over old gouges, down
to hiding in the filthy toilet long enough
to visualize the naked pinups arching
and swelling on the fleshy wall
above the workbench, and to study the moldy
Sir and *Swank* girlie pages always stashed
behind the stench of the water tank;
and coming out a man, skin scoured red
with Lava soap, then perfumed clean
by sweet, gray mechanic's slime, imagining
my muscles and veins cabled like his.

Getting down, that is, to liking it,
like my first black coffee with shots
of I.W. Harper at my elbow on the Alcazar bar,
yelling for his shuffleboard lags, twenty-dollar bills

almost his on the whispery-fast golden wood—
and finally, going home, if he's not just drunk
but *really* drunk, he lets me steer from my side of the seat
as he keeps gunning the gas and braking suddenly,
betting me all the money he owes me
I can't keep us from crashing.

4.

I'm peering now from the dark back end of the Arrow
    Garage
toward the far front doors swung open and
daylight dimming in from lower Telegraph.
I've made such little progress all this time,
barely past the twisted chain-hoist where
a frozen engine's been suspended all my life,
still back with the acid turning
solid and cold in the hot-dip tank.

The world of ashen light out there
seems too many mass-extinctions away,
and the scraper itself is scrap in my hands.
So now, perhaps, much more than enough
is finally enough—while I can still unbend
off this floor, joints grating, fist in my chest
still punching—enough to let me say
in whatever voice is left me: Enough,
enough of this shit. I quit.

Smoke of My Own Breath *is published in an edition of 1,000 copies, 26 of which have been lettered and signed by the author for friends of Garlic Press.*

Garlic Press
483 S. Kirkwood Road
#13
St. Louis, MO 63122

Peter Genovese, Editor & Publisher

Cover Art: Kevin Belford
Design: Patricia Clewell